Is

PUBLIC HEALTH

More Important Than Personal Freedom?

By Layla Owens

Published in 2023 by
KidHaven Publishing, an Imprint of Greenhaven Publishing, LLC
29 E. 21st Street
New York, NY 10010

Designer: Deanna Paternostro
Editor: Caitie McAneney

Photo credits: Cover Dipta Subhra Sarkar/Shutterstock.com; pp. 5, 21 (inset, middle) FamVeld/Shutterstock.com; pp. 7, 11 Ilyas Tayfun Salci/Shutterstock.com; p. 9 Rido/Shutterstock.com; p. 13 Tom Wang/Shutterstock.com; p. 15 Alexander_Safonov/Shutterstock.com; p. 17 Noiel/Shutterstock.com; p. 19 Bihlmayer Fotografie/Shutterstock.com; p. 21 (notepad) ESB Professional/Shutterstock.com; p. 21 (markers) Kucher Serhii/Shutterstock.com; p. 21 (photo frame) FARBAI/iStock/Thinkstock; p. 21 (inset, left) Halfpoint/Shutterstock.com; p. 21 (inset, right) IHOR SULYATYTSKYY/Shutterstock.com.

Library of Congress Cataloging-in-Publication Data

Names: Owens, Layla, author.
Title: Is public health more important than personal freedom? / Layla
  Owens.
Description: New York : KidHaven Publishing, [2023] | Series: Points of
  view | Includes index.
Identifiers: LCCN 2021048329 (print) | LCCN 2021048330 (ebook) | ISBN
  9781534541917 (library binding) | ISBN 9781534541894 (paperback) | ISBN
  9781534541900 (set) | ISBN 9781534541924 (ebook)
Subjects: LCSH: Public health–Juvenile literature. | Debates and
  debating–Juvenile literature. | Vaccines–Juvenile literature. |
  Quarantine–Juvenile literature.
Classification: LCC RA425 .O88 2023 (print) | LCC RA425 (ebook) | DDC
  362.1–dc23/eng/20211104
LC record available at https://lccn.loc.gov/2021048329
LC ebook record available at https://lccn.loc.gov/2021048330

Printed in the United States of America

Some of the images in this book illustrate individuals who are models. The depictions do not imply actual situations or events.

CPSIA compliance information: Batch #CSKH23: For further information contact Greenhaven Publishing LLC, New York, New York at 1-844-317-7404.

Please visit our website, www.greenhavenpublishing.com. For a free color catalog of all our high-quality books, call toll free 1-844-317-7404 or fax 1-844-317-7405.

Find us on

CONTENTS

What Is
PUBLIC HEALTH?

Think of the last time you were sick. Maybe you made the hard decision to stay home from school. Maybe it was for your personal health, so you could rest and recover. But it might have also been for public health.

Public health helps and protects the health of people in a community. It means trying to keep people from getting sick or hurt. Some people believe public health is everyone's responsibility, or duty. They support public health **mandates** to keep the public safe. Other people believe their only responsibility is to their own body. They value personal freedom.

Know the Facts!

The first major public health law was the Public Health Act of 1848. It made rules about the **conditions** of England and Wales to try to prevent illness.

Some people say arguments around public health are a matter between life and death.

Pandemic
PROBLEMS

Contagious illnesses have been around for many thousands of years. From smallpox to influenza (the flu), viruses have killed millions of people throughout history. Many viruses have been wiped out thanks to public health measures like vaccines. Others still affect people today.

In 2019, a deadly virus was found in Wuhan, China. Named COVID-19, it swept through the world by 2020. Many people had a fever, cough, and trouble breathing. By July 2021, 4 million people had died from the pandemic. Governments tried to put public health measures in place, such as mandating masks and developing vaccines.

Know the Facts!

By September 2021, 1 in 500 Americans had died from COVID-19.

COVID-19 brought the public health **debate** to the spotlight. Some people pushed back against public health measures.

Life-Saving
VACCINES

A vaccine is often given in a shot. It trains your **immune system** to create antibodies. Antibodies are chemicals in the body that fight the virus. Then, your body will know how to fight the virus if you are around it. This often keeps you from spreading the virus, too.

A COVID-19 vaccine became widely available in the United States in 2021. It was free and scientists said it was safe. Many people said that it was a person's duty to take the vaccine. It could stop the spread of COVID-19 and keep people safe, especially older adults and children.

Know the Facts!

Vaccines have been very **effective** in the fight against COVID-19. They keep people from getting very sick or dying.

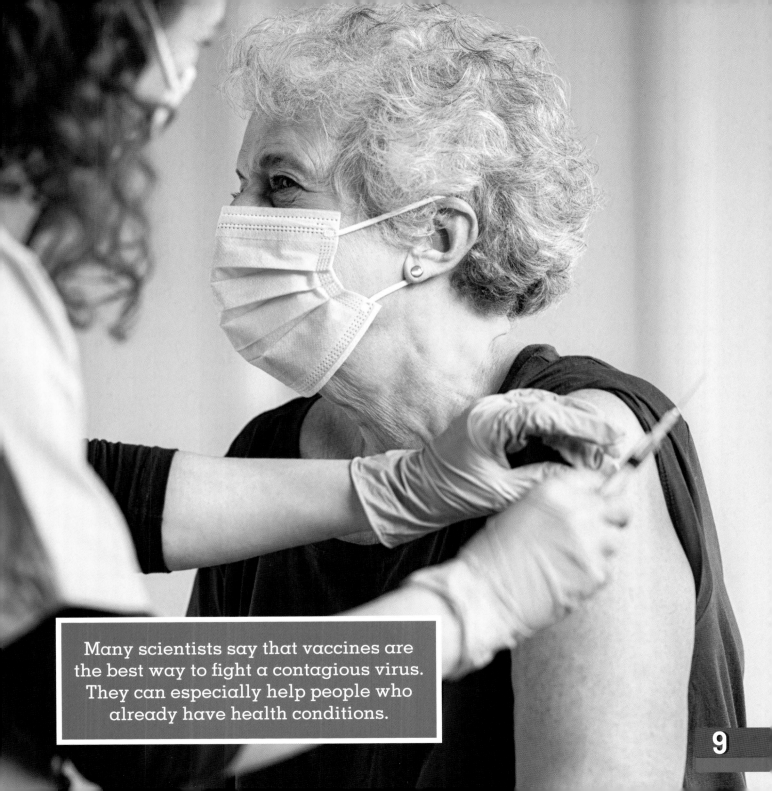

Many scientists say that vaccines are the best way to fight a contagious virus. They can especially help people who already have health conditions.

My Body,
MY CHOICE

Some people are against vaccines. They don't think the vaccines are safe or effective. Some believe a report (which was proven untrue) that there's a link between childhood vaccines and **autism**. They believe that they should be able to choose what they put into their body.

While many people saw a vaccine as a life-saving step in ending COVID-19, other people pushed against the idea of vaccine mandates. They say that personal freedom is more important than public health. Some don't think the vaccines have been tested enough. They don't trust scientists. Some don't believe COVID-19 is real or serious.

Know the Facts!

According to a June 2021 Gallup Poll, about 1 in 5 Americans did not plan to get vaccinated for COVID-19.

Many people see vaccine mandates as a sign that the government has too much control.

Mask UP!

When COVID-19 hit the United States, many state governments put mask mandates in place. That meant people had to wear a mask in public places, such as stores, doctor's offices, and event spaces.

Scientists say that wearing masks is an effective way of stopping the spread of virus. The mask acts as a barrier, or wall, between the mouth and nose of an infected person and the people around them. It keeps particles, or bits, of virus from spreading. Many people believe everyone should wear masks in public. It is a safe and easy way to keep others safe.

Know the Facts!

A June 2020 study found that the growth rates of COVID-19 cases declined after face mask mandates were set in 15 states plus Washington, D.C. in April and May 2020.

In some parts of Asia, such as China, wearing a mask when you feel sick is common. It's a way to keep other people safe and stop the spread of sickness.

Masks as
MUZZLES

Some people believe being forced to wear a mask is a sign that personal freedoms are being taken away. They even call masks "muzzles," comparing them to face coverings that keep dogs from biting. They believe it's their choice to wear or not wear a mask.

Some people think that masks aren't an effective way to protect against COVID-19. They say that masks can actually make people think they're safe when they're not. They say that masks can harm people who have difficulty breathing due to health issues. Some people think wearing a mask makes them look weak or scared.

Know the Facts!

Mask mandates make it harder for some people with hearing loss to communicate. Many people with hearing loss depend on reading lips.

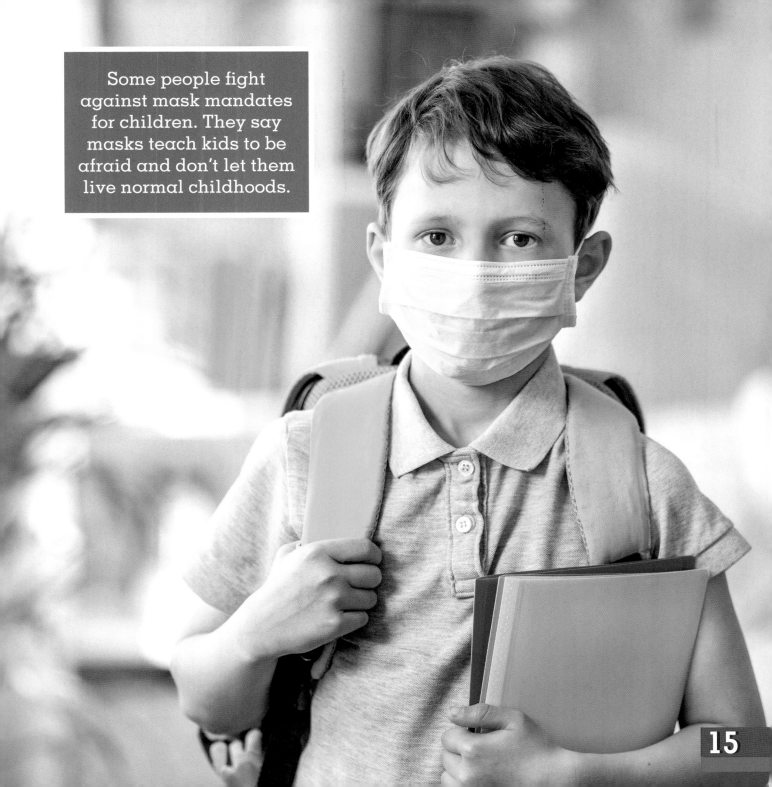

Some people fight against mask mandates for children. They say masks teach kids to be afraid and don't let them live normal childhoods.

Taking
ACTION

Many people support taking any action that can stop the spread of a virus, such as testing, tracking, and **quarantines**. Testing a person for illness helps doctors find out what's making them sick so they can treat it. It also helps doctors and scientists track viruses as they spread. Then, governments can take the best actions to keep the public safe, such as making people stay home.

Many people think testing is important. Even though COVID tests can be uncomfortable, they give important information. People say if a person could be sick, they should stay away from others.

Know the Facts!

The Centers for Disease Control and Prevention (CDC) has a COVID data tracker that tells people how many cases of COVID-19 are in their area.

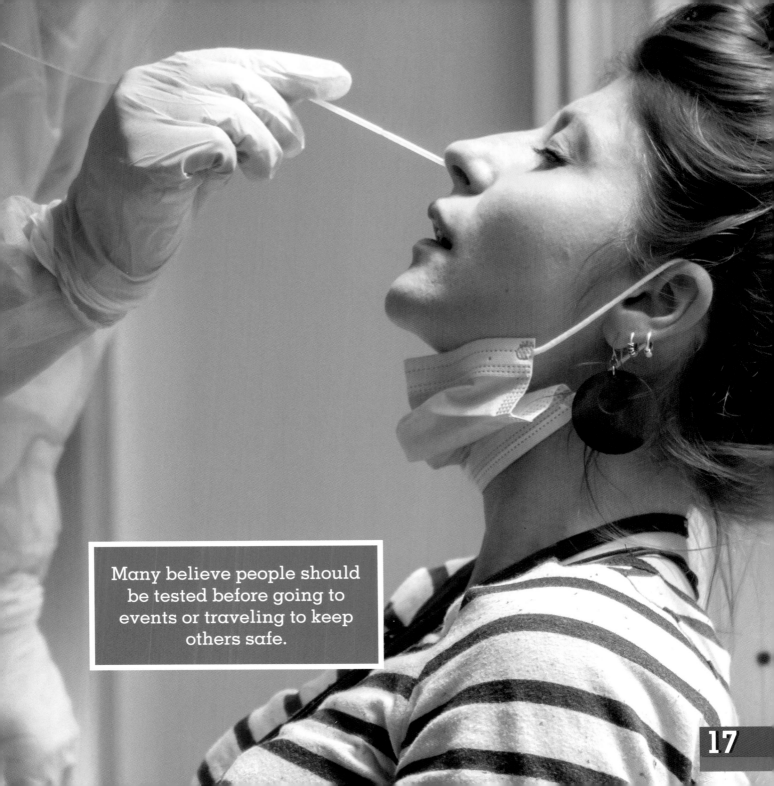

Many believe people should be tested before going to events or traveling to keep others safe.

17

Freedom to MOVE

Many governments made rules that kept people from traveling or going to public places at the beginning of the COVID-19 pandemic. Countries and states limited who could travel there. Places like restaurants and hair salons were closed. Many people were upset that they lost their businesses and their jobs. Children couldn't go to school.

Some people thought these rules went against their freedom. They wanted to be able to travel. They didn't want the government to mandate testing or tell them to stay home. They wanted to go to work and school. They wanted to go out to eat or get a haircut.

Know the Facts!

About 9.6 million U.S. workers lost their jobs in 2020.

Many business owners were angry that they had to close their doors during COVID-19. Some even lost their businesses.

What's More
IMPORTANT?

The debate between public health and personal freedom became very important during the COVID-19 pandemic. Many of the arguments had to do with young people.

Some people argued that children should be able to go back to school because time away would hurt their education. Other people argued that children should stay home and learn over the computer to keep themselves and others safe. Some people wanted children to wear masks to school, while other people argued that wearing masks was uncomfortable and scary. What do you think is more important: public health or personal freedom?

Know the Facts!

Misinformation is wrong information that is spread about something. Misinformation about COVID-19 made it hard for people to know what was factual.

Is public health more important than personal freedom?

YES

- Vaccines are effective ways to keep people safe, especially people at risk of dying.

- Mask mandates can help keep a virus from spreading.

- Taking action against a virus is the only way to keep people from dying.

- Children should stay home from school to keep themselves and others safe.

NO

- A person should be able to choose if they want a vaccine.

- A person should have the freedom to choose if they want to wear a mask.

- A person should be able to go where they want to go without being tested.

- Keeping children out of school hurts their education.

The debates around public health and personal freedom can be heated. It's important to look at both sides.

21

GLOSSARY

autism: A disorder in which a person may have trouble communicating and socializing with others.

condition: The way things are at a time or in a place.

contagious: Able to spread infection or disease from one being to another.

debate: An argument or discussion about an issue, generally between two sides.

develop: To create something or to cause something to become more advanced.

effective: Producing a wanted result.

immune system: The parts of the body that fight germs and keep it healthy.

mandate: An official order to do something.

pandemic: An outbreak of disease that occurs over a wide geographic area and affects a great proportion of the population.

quarantine: Keeping someone away from the public to stop the spread of disease.

vaccine: A shot that keeps a person from getting a certain sickness.

virus: A very small living thing that causes disease and spreads from one person or animal to another.

For More
INFORMATION

WEBSITES

Facts About Coronavirus

kids.nationalgeographic.com/science/article/facts-about-coronavirus
What exactly is COVID-19? This helpful article from National Geographic
Kids will give you the facts.

A Kid's Guide to Shots

kidshealth.org/en/kids/guide-shots.html#catbody
Learn more about how vaccines can keep you safe from illness
with KidsHealth.

BOOKS

Keppeler, Jill. *Pandemics: COVID-19 and Our World*. New York, NY:
PowerKids Press, 2022.

Macgregor, Eloise. *Be a Virus Warrior! A Kid's Guide to Keeping Safe*. New
York, NY: PowerKids Press, 2020.

Mayer, Melissa. *The Micro World of Viruses and Bacteria*. North Mankato,
MN: Capstone Press, 2022.

INDEX